BLEEDING GHOSTS

BLEEDING GHOSTS
© Lara Chamoun / Cathexis Northwest Press

No part of this book may be reproduced without written permission
of the publisher or author, except in reviews and articles.

First Printing: 2025

ISBN: 979-8-9928991-1-5

Cover Image: Attraction by Edvard Munch, Art Institute of Chicago
Editing & Design by C. M. Tollefson
Cathexis Northwest Press
cathexisnorthwestpress.com

BLEEDING GHOSTS

LARA CHAMOUN

Cathexis Northwest Press

"You may not believe in magic but something very strange is happening at this very moment. Your head has dissolved into thin air and I can see the rhododendrons through your stomach. It's not that you are dead or anything dramatic like that, it is simply that you are fading away and I can't even remember your name."

— Leonora Carrington, *The Hearing Trumpet*

TABLE OF CONTENTS

I. Flesh and Bone

II. Affections

III. Hauntings

IV. Flesh and Metal

V. Erasure

I. FLESH AND BONE

THE SCAR

Before the cave drawings spoke your name and the bones beneath your skin began to hum, there was the scar. Before your mother's hands became tools of excavation, unearthing splinters from your flesh; before the empty spaces between the stars at night began to stretch and sag with the weight of the things you forgot, like that favourite toy ball you lost, there was the scar. You trace its rough edges in your flesh, its ridge a worn fossil, and it undulates beneath your fingerprint and pulses warmth. You shift in the night, in the creases of your bedsheets, to where the fabric is cooler, to where your skin is smooth, almost slick.

Before the sand scattered and the tides licked the shore, the moon guiding them to erase your footprints, there was the scar. Before the wild-eyed man with pockets full of teeth, before your wisdom teeth, before the tooth fairy and your baby teeth, before they promised to make you whole again, you wandered into a forest and reached down hollow trunks. Before that there was the scar, and it felt like bark as you pressed your fingers to it, the story carved into your skin. You whittled a spear and hunted a doe, you tore into it with your bare teeth, and before that there was the scar.

Before the valley swallowed you whole and before there were flowers, before your choking bounced off stone walls and sunk into the ground, before there were ashes and before your father's voice slackened to leather and you nearly set fire to the leather couch, there was the scar. There was the scar under your leather jacket, there was the scar under your jean jacket, your winter jacket, your raincoat. You could see it right through the fabric; you could trace it in its creases. You couldn't forget it on the surface because it was so persistent.

Before the sky turned to stone and the ground crumbled, there was the scar in the way you walked with your arm bent like a fish hook, with your leg bending with it. It was there, in the lilt of your voice as you asked for cookies, for a kiss, for a few more minutes. It was there in the curve of your neck when you tilted your head to ask why.

Before the gaps between the clouds began to widen and before sleep became a distant memory, the scar became a distant memory, laying quiet like the space

5

between your breaths. It faded like a whisper after your first words squeezed through your throat, slimy and strangled. There was the scar before your first words; before you discovered you could mimic the sound of raindrops on the window; before you learned interpretative dance with kitchen utensils and the most creative uses for rubber bands; before you named every squirrel in the neighbourhood and rescued a family of ducks from a storm drain; before you learned to decipher the patterns of moss growth on old buildings and realised they all looked like your family; before you took a plastic pail and shovel into your backyard and dug until you found a fossil that was really a stick; before the scar was bleeding flesh that gravel had bitten the first time you fell from your bicycle.

THE TATTOO

Every Thursday morning the tattoo was a fractured mirror, and you traced the frame of the glass in front of you as your eyes followed the carousel. The scar beneath it tingled. It was once in the vacant lot in between your house and the park, the one with unicorns and dragons that spun endlessly until one day when you came to visit from college. It glittered in circles: it was dust through a window on a stale day; the feeling of laughter that wasn't yours rippling your skin. You hated the carousel every time it came around, the unicorns and dragons with empty saddles around your upper arm, into the blue of your bruise. It hurt when you pressed it; it made the ink animals fade for a moment, before reappearing in your armpit where you couldn't see them. You kept pressing so that the bruise would stay, to remind you of some stranger's grief as the pictures pulled away and around. You felt some kind of nostalgia in the movement, some echoing of xylophone.

By noon the breeze coming through an open window stirs your bedroom and forms silver spoons that clink together on their invisible thread. It's there, taut around your arm, pressing the bruise into a thin line where the carousel unfurled into the stainless steel mirrors. You can see your face in their round back and recognize some stranger with a chill.

The spoons turn to sand, and the grains seem to scratch an itch you didn't really have before. They all pool below your windowsill and scatter across the floorboards like little vanishing deserts, always slipping between the cracks. They're little vanishing deserts like rotting fruit and melting clocks. The sand turns to liquid glass that drips from your skin and soothes an ache hidden in a freckle with rain-shaped hieroglyphics. Something that never fully formed clings to a vein and clots. There's more blue, like bluebells blooming under a child's skin.

Then there are tangled threads like a window after rain, cheeks after being pressed to something honeyed and glazed. It's night and there are constellations, there is purple after blue and oceans with phosphorescent jellyfish that sting. They pulse in your bed sheets that were not tucked quite right under your mattress and come loose, you tentacle in them until the wrinkles are right and they press a deep spot of tenderness.

The Taste of Metal

You bit your tongue and a coppery taste flooded you. You were five, maybe six, and you paused with the pain, clamped your mouth shut, and remained in your confusion as the metallic tang lingered and the ache spread into it. You pressed your tongue to the roof of your mouth, ran it over the uneven edges of emerging teeth and in the gaps where some had fallen out, from when you tripped in the grass or knocked your head on an easel. The scar bristled because it remembered too.

You tested the limits of your flesh by chewing on paper clips, and learned to spit them when they snapped and savour the slight cut. The taste was hot without warmth, sharp without an edge, something like the shape of lighting, a summer storm and its innards. Your tongue would swell and fill your throat and there was some kind of electric hum.

At parties, you tilted your glass and pulled your lips upwards to meet the cold rim of a glass, hoping for it to stick, to coat your mouth fully, for some kind of reminder. When there was no ache you forgot everything except the satisfaction. Wine trickled down your throat in small sips like velvet, deep and cold, like ice to a wound. When the pressure disappeared there was a dull throb of exasperation.

On your bed, legs swinging above the carpet, you pressed coins to your tongue. One after the other from a little pouch of old tooth fairy money from which you kept tossing to the people who slept over the grates on the sidewalk. The coins tasted like licking tree roots, so you bit down and spit them out with freshly stained lips like they were pebbles. The copper penny tasted like history, like the one you were going to have. You learned the texture of metal on the edges of tin cans, the clasp of your necklace, the wire of your braces. Then the blood would come, warm and fusible, to trace a path with your tongue, landmarking. You gnawed the end of a pen until ink exploded in your mouth, you licked the railing on a staircase on a dare and felt the cold against you, tasted rust and salt for days afterwards.

You pressed your tongue to the back of your teeth, to the arc of grooves and ridges where the enamel had worn away. You found pockets of the metallic taste between your gums, and the taste became permanent, coated every meal and every word. Sometimes you coughed up blood. In the kitchen, you held a spoon against your tongue and felt it absorb the warmth of it cradled. You kept a box of trinkets and tools with different flavours: a paperclip was rain-soaked pavement and a safety pin was a trodden leaf in autumn. Each cut formed a catalogue. You pressed a key to your tongue and old locks, forgotten doors, rusted tang tasted like a secret.

You carried a tin whistle and placed it between your teeth to feel the thrum of its hollow body meet yours, your heartbeat. When you're stuck in traffic you bite the inside of your cheek and you realise it tastes like memories of scraped elbows. You bite down harder, welcoming the flood.

THE CRYING

The crying began like wind slipping through the cracks of an old window, like the cool pressure of whistling through a missing tooth. It was faint, almost imperceptible, a bit of a whimper, distant, something that should've been easy to ignore. You moved to open your window and slam it shut again, you expected the paint to chip and to not bother repainting it. You did not expect it to be forced open by the crying, louder, more insistent, like a rusty hinge swinging back and forth.

You lay in bed and wondered as the noise pressed into your scar like gravel, traced your tattoo like laughter. It was a cat trapped somewhere it shouldn't be. It was the neighbour's baby. It slipped under the bedroom door and crept closer to you. You felt it curl against your own crescent-moon form in your bedsheets, and you cradled it, thrashing, as it thread your thoughts into a loop, the limits of your tangled limbs. There was a pressure in your stomach where it settled, and there was a gnawing hunger.

You made your way down the hall and dipped a cookie in a glass of milk. The crying didn't stop, it was still hungry, and in the dim kitchen lights you could almost see it, an infant with eyes the size of its mouth and tiny hands that pinched and pinched. It blinked and you felt the gaps between your bones. It looked like what you'd imagined in your child: vagueness, ghostliness, something that could've been.

It clawed at your ears in the silence of your office between the taps on the keyboard, the hum of the fridge you hadn't yet fixed, the loose spring on the couch when you sat down to watch a soap opera and the slosh of wine in your stained glass. You drank it like it was something wrong, like a miscarriage or the reason why you could feel your ribs grate your skin when you would breathe in too deeply.

At night the cries filled the room and pressed against your eardrums, it now cradled you with nails digging in your skin as it towered over the bed. The bedboard creaked its own cries as it snapped, and you clutched your pillow, trying to replace something, as your mattress met the floor. The threads of your limbs together in your head went taut. There were earplugs and there was music and there was a loud distorted wailing.

You rocked the infant as the cries reached a fever pitch, and your arms curled around the empty space. You murmured soft half-words, some soothing babble because you couldn't manage anything more. Your throat was hoarse and you sucked your thumb. You bit it, it bled and tasted like growth. You wrapped your blanket around yourself and noticed it was stained.

In the kitchen you brought a spoon to your mouth and nursed it with your tongue as their crescent-moon shapes met each other. You hummed and offered a taste to the air and it cooed in between bawls. A mush of nonsense trickled down your chin to your fuzzy rabbit shirt. You curled up on the couch and brought your knees to your chest and rocked to the rhythm of the crying.

THE BONE COLLECTOR

When light is dimmed by amnesia, you'll gather bones by searching for detached echoes: they're scattered like the places where reverberations are gathered in alcoves. Look for indifferent objects; look under piles of dead leaves; look beside lost pennies; look next to moth-eaten shawls. You'll find a rib in the dust of a carousel's creaking; you'll see that it has a surface like old wood that pocketed laughter fallen between its cracks. You'll find a scapula beneath a rusted swing with a sagging smile, slick from the residue of the sugar and dew in the air. You'll find the collarbone curled around sandcastles and crumbling plastic pails, shimmering like the deserts after a sprinkling of liquid glass. You'll have this gnawing hunger for phosphorescent pain.

You'll find a rib on the pews of a filthy church, you'll find it stained with bruises like mould and humming in the silence of rotting glass. You'll catch this muted reminder of hymns and crying around your restless limbs. You'll find a phalanx in the threads of a spider's web that tastes of rain-soaked tin. You'll find a skull on a stage with a flimsy cardboard set in an empty auditorium. Alas, poor you; you knew her well. You'll lift it and find it weighs a poem, have it face its phantom audience and ask for a joke.

You'll find a rib wrapped in the patterns of a quilt, you'll embrace it and feel it stab your stomach with some kind of softness. You'll find an ulna in a folded yellow map with dots of ink like footsteps, leading to someplace drawn wrong because once upon a time it hadn't been properly discovered. You'll find the sternum flat and centre in a bouquet of flaking brown roses, tinged with a sweetness like decay, bruising you like a festering fruit.

You'll arrange the bones on a wooden-echo table beneath a soft red and light and watch them form the silhouette of a timeless ego; you'll notice the familiar bite of gravel and your escape from the darkroom: the cold metal of bicycle handlebars that once burned. You'll run your entire withered arm across it and remember the ache of a small wound's permanence.

II. Affections

THE WHISPER

You shift in your bed into some liquid shadow, to where your sheets are cooler, and the whisper drifts towards you. There it is: a lover's breath that settles on your cheek and warms you, a whisper like silk sliding over your bare legs, an embrace without a touch. The moon's edge sharpens the air between you.

The voice is soft and murmurs love against the contours of your ears, drapes you in the delight of this secret that clings to your skin like a lover's kiss lingering in the empty spaces between your faded thoughts. The whisper unfurls like petals on your pulse, flushes the edges of your pining with a pressure as lonely as moonlight dancing on a lover's bare skin. It caresses your scar, traces it like it's reading an old story dulled in the moonlight but brought to life by the sound.

You close your eyes and that lover's breath traces paths across your eyelids and between your lashes. You feel something oscillate beneath them. There is warm silk like a murmur slipping through your fingers, you are wrapped in a sweet aching as the nighttime folds over you like velvety curtains drawing closed. It comes with this satiny goading against the blackness, a memory pulled tight around the edges of your vision; there is a whisper of gentle insistence as you drift away.

The whisper beats in your chest to the steps of a slow dance around the contours of your wakefulness, breathing life into the fantasies of a different daily life that flits beneath your closed lids. They flicker like little candles in the corners of your mind, on the brink of your waking thoughts. They weave through them delicately and pull you deeper.

The whisper traces lines of white caps as your consciousness dips. In the darkness your whole body sighs and it lingers, holding you in its quiet clutches. Your dreams drown in the whisper, unintelligible words rippling in still water. Something spreads and you want it.

The murmur wraps itself around you and holds itself there like mist, curls into the nape of your neck. You feel the chill of someone tracing the curve of your spine, sending shivers that melt into the whisper's warmth. The whisper fills the room and presses on your thoughts and widens their gaps.

You are drawn into the dance; the whisper leads, you follow, step by step and deeper. Your bed fades into the touch of the mumbling that surrounds you and marks you and flatters you; fits you perfectly, weaves longing behind closed eyes, a web that draws you close.

The air grows thick and stifling as the moon fades, the heady scent of moonflower becoming stale. A golden line seems to form in the crook of your window frame, turns to a frigid breath that chills your bare skin and seeps through the blanket that you pull over yourself. The embrace constricts, mist and threads tightening around you and squeezing breath from your lungs as you cough dust. The whisper echoes in the empty space where you should've been able to take someone's warm hand and rest a kiss.

THE MANNEQUIN

You find her in an attic somewhere, porcelain skin glinting in the half-light, wearing a dress of dust, and you wonder if you've ever been a tailor. You recall the dust, but not holding a thread. Her painted eyes are close to glinting, the colour of emeralds, because of course an artist would forget that eyes are never that green. Her lips are taut, in a line so straight that the feeling behind your eyes tries to bend their tips upwards.

You bring her home in a downpour, drape her in your plastic yellow poncho. You have to pause to raise the hood over her smooth oval head when you realise that the paint from her eyes is running. Her neck is so slender that you worry just the weight of the yellow plastic will snap it. The rest of her doesn't need a raincoat; you laugh as the droplets slide right off her because she'll feel nothing. You shiver all the way home.

You share your first meal at breakfast time, and you prop her up at the table with cereal boxes. She stares at you, lips slightly parted, as you let porridge settle in your stomach. She listens to you chew with fiberglass ears, barely hinted at by her perfectly formed head. This bothered you. It must've bothered her too, she was crying: paint tracks meshed with rain stain her cheeks.

Every day now you brush her hair: you chose from your closet the fluffiest wig, dark hair to conceal her unfinished ears. You're very careful to place her hair to hide any unfinished touches. Every day you paint her nails a different colour, every day your hands tremble a bit less. The first day was your first time holding a bottle of nail polish, a tiny bottle of nail polish, you were scared of breaking it as you brought her stiff fingers into your palm and imagined the contours of her cuticles with the little brush. Every day now you dress her in the sequined dresses and feather boas and heels that dominate your closet. You wear the oversized grey sweater and worn jeans and scruffed shoes. She joins you in the living room and poses gracefully as you slouch, you grasp her hand and mould yours to fit between her fingers perfectly. You watch old movies and let the popcorn sprinkle across her lap.

You bring her to dinner parties, double-dates with your friends, and explain that she's the perfect listener, a date that won't need small talk. You introduce her as Marianne and laugh so that they will too. You push her on a swing at the park and laugh to match the children's giggles. You move her leg to just the right angle to craft a memory. In your workshop, you sculpt her smile and chisel away at the old wood. You don't do a very good job: now that she's smiling she's mocking. You're not very good at crafting gestures of affection.

One evening, you dress her in the wedding gown buried in the back of your closet, making sure her veil hides her ears. You dance in the living room with your bride and twirl to a song that only you and maybe the cockroaches can hear, gently grasping the ungiving arm around your neck.

That night, you tuck her into bed and read her poetry about love. You stop when your words begin to echo and she's still crying her painted tears. Why was she still crying? You did what you were supposed to. You trace the perfect lines of her face and wish they were familiar, longing for a warmth that once graced your fingertips.

THE REFLECTION

You find yourself enamoured with the fact that her eyes aren't quite your own, and they twinkle in the glass like a second heartbeat. You stand transfixed as she smoothes her hair with a grace that seems almost like serenity. She applies her makeup with practised precision, the mirror framing her face like artwork. You're in a museum; you stand close to the painting but don't dare reach out.

You speak to her in quiet moments, and your words bounce back foreign. Her lips part and her responses reverberate in your head. Each morning you stand before the mirror and watch as she dresses in your clothes, the nice ones in the back of closets that you've saved forever for a special occasion. You watch her craft herself with something you don't understand. You can't seem to mimic the way she moves like water flowing around stones. She smiles as if to invite you to step beyond the glass.

You place your hand against the cool surface and let your smudged handprint settle there as she matches your gesture. You're palm to palm and the glass shivers between your touch. Your heartbeat matches hers, your pulse meets hers, and if you close your eyes you are mirrors together.

In the dark hours she steps outside the mirror. You share your meals with her and set your coffee table for two. She laughs at your jokes and she joins you in bed. You feel her breath on your neck as you slip into sleep, and when you wake she knows your secrets. She's coaxed them out of you, one by one, whispering them back from your dreams with the same delicate care she uses to handle her hairbrush. You notice that with each one she looks more dishevelled.

Before the sun rises, in a civil sort of twilight, you watch drowsily as she emerges from your closet in a gown you've never seen before. She smiles lopsidedly as the light begins to filter in through the curtains like she's just remembered a life you've forgotten, or maybe never lived at all.

You're trapped in the mirror when it shatters at dawn-break.

THE GHOST KISS

There is a whispering in between your footsteps and the floorboards as you make your way through the hall. You sense a lover's touch on your skin as you open the fridge for a glass of milk. There she is. You see yourself swallowed by the absence of light in her sockets. You wave both to her and to yourself, and you wonder if your hands would seem more worn than hers if you could see them. They're cold and damp as they guide you to the old, stained loveseat.

She moves closer, blending with the cushion and your shadow on the yellow fabric. Her lips are pale; you do not see them. You feel her in the air first, shivering, and she's already halfway there. Her touch is so piercing you feel a fire lit somewhere in your stomach and it crawls its way up your throat. You lean in and breathe in the glass.

Her kiss seeps so deeply into your bones that you're sure no blanket or hearth can save you. All you have is your fire. Static moves down your spine and you contort to meet her shape, there is nothing soft about this subtlety. It's liquid nitrogen falling around chocolate-dipped strawberries, freezing them into hearts. It's not being able to pay the bill for that night, too elegant for both of you. It's nothing like quiet cafés or split coffee. Her fingers trace your jawline as you tremble.

You lose yourself to this reality, more tangible than a movie theatre and sharing popcorn with a stranger, more palpable than a carnival and a kiss atop a Ferris wheel. Her kiss deepens and she tastes like the droplets of water that gather on mirrors, like an iced cucumber drink with rose petals on top. It's closer than a beach at sunset or the perfect park bench.

In the dim light of the living room, you find her nestled against you, and she's the most undeniable feeling. You stand and move to the mirror and expect her to follow, but she remains there, still and limp. You touch your lips and they feel foreign, they crease like a petal curls; she's sculpted herself into you.

You go to smooth your hair with a grace that seems almost like serenity, and put on the nicest clothes in the back of your closet. As you step into the hallway you feel her whisper warm your ear, you feel a hand-breeze brush your shoulder. You wear the weight of your affections and pull your lips upward.

III. Hauntings

THE DOPPELGÄNGER'S DIARY

You find the diary yellowed in the drawer of a grandfather clock, buried in a velvet cloth and peppermint candies. Its cover is embossed with golden curls, ringlets, exotic vines that spell your name if maybe you were a blond and a princess. The ink smells something like stardust-infused caramel moonlight with a hint of metallic nostalgia.

First, you read about a carousel ride with golden trapeze swings. You remember that day, you rode in a swan-shaped hot air balloon while sweat soaked your sun hat shaped like a swan's bill. Now, as you read, you're spinning in a tuxedo stitched from stardust and you're collecting raindrops in an opal teacup and it's wrong. Tuxedo-You's back isn't curved quite enough, someone who's her still sits beside them on that swan-ride Tuxedo-You is missing a weight. This was your birthday and that afternoon in that sun hat you ate chocolate cake with red frosting; the page ends by stating that Tuxedo-You had vanilla cake with blue. You stare through time at the frosting as if it might taste different, but it only feels like another thing you can't touch.

Then it's a nighttime picnic on the field of pendulums and you're drinking clouds that taste like sugar and the sky. You remember it was daytime, you remember you felt okay sampling velvet mushrooms alone because of this. But in these pages Cloud-You longs while clutching her hand, pointing, wanting for the candy-coated comets that keep crashing into the play structure. You're the one left longing, watching her from a distance as you savour a moment you no longer share. She haunts the margins of these recollections without her and you trace the velvet cloth for a hint of mushroom. Cloud-You doesn't seem to know what it's like to have those comets fall silent, to lose the taste of the blue heavens on your tongue.

Then it's the masquerade ball at the local floating library, and cloaked in a moonbeam, Moon-You rides up on a goldfish wearing a gown made of a language you don't speak. You remember that you had to fly there with book pages like butterfly wings and that you wore a suit made of whispers. The diary describes a waltz with chivalrous ghosts, but you only recall your arguments with the time-travelling librarians. Moon-You never argues; they simply sway, hand in hers, and they dance to and through languages you never learned.

Then you shift to a zephyr-powered zeppelin floating through a fog shaped like a kaleidoscope. You see yourself in the fog as a child riding a magical carousel; you remember imagining this in a sandbox. Adult-You lounges amidst the haze, sipping from a goblet of gold, flicking their wrist elegantly as the sun frames them. There's an ease in that flick, a kind of grace you can't quite replicate, almost like serenity. You look away, through the pages and deep into the future of yourself where you are reaching out for the her you lost here. Adult-You watches the sandbox and takes a swig and sighs into the air the weight of who you haven't yet met.

Finally you're at the bizarre bazaar, and you remember rushing around with slowly freezing hands, dragging her behind you as you traded gold for time – a pocket watch ticking backwards and a wristwatch that struck eighteen. You bartered with the glass-eyed vendors as she slipped from your fingers, leaving nothing but a leftover chill because the paths of your palm were now bare and frozen over. You slumped with the weight of them and let them graze the ground lovingly. Bazaar-You trades easily, your hand never slipping from her grasp. You move through time losing only what you choose to forget.

You never raise your head from the pages to realise you're standing alone. That Other-You is gone and your hand is tracing the golden embossing of the diary's spine. You don't close the book to seal away this life that could've been yours. You hide it in your closet near the wedding dress, your fingers stained with golden ink to remind you that it's not.

THE ECHO CHAMBER

"Hello?"
"Umbrella."

"What?"
"Moonlight."

"Are you serious?"
"Blueberries."

"This place is weird."
"Cosmic."

"Maybe I'm just tired."
"Fireworks."

"I'll get used to it."
"Paradox."

"This isn't funny."
"Requiem."

"Okay, this is enough."
"Catastrophe."

"Why?"
"Candlewax."

"Why are you doing this?"
"Needle."

"I'm fine. I'm fine."
"Jigsaw."

"She should be here."
"Constellation."

"Where is she?"
"Saffron."

"I want her back."
"Phantom."

"I need her back."
"Lavender."

"Why did she leave?"
"Echo."

"No, no, that's not it."
"Alchemy."

"What is this place doing to me?"
"Carousel."

"This place isn't going to break me."
"Resonance."

"I'll find her and the truth together."
"Ellipsis."

"I'm still here."
"Butterfly."

"I won't let you win."
"Honeycomb."

"No, I'm not."
"Puzzle."

"Please, just stop."
"Mirage."

"I miss her."
"Apricot."

"I'm coming for you."
"Watch."

"I'm afraid."
"Scar."

"Where?"

Mirror mirror mirror

THE FUNHOUSE

You're inside the funhouse and you remember every frame. One is from your house now, the bathroom, one is from your childhood home and one is from the red-brick, white-picket house you've imagined and never seen. You can almost remember what's behind the glass.

The frame is a bicycle handle. You see yourself at the edge of the carousel on your upper arm, not riding a golden trapeze swing but clutching your side, fingers pressing against the scar in the pit of your bruise, running over the dents that playground gravel left. You hold onto it here like a medal for a fight you never fought.

You move forward, but the mirrors match your pace. The frame is a ribcage. You see yourself hunched over, collecting bones in your echo-room. You hear their hollow in the pit of your stomach as you watch yourself drop them one by one into a velvet bag. You remember the attic filled with whispers, a familiar voice leading you to a small female skull underneath a cobweb. But in this reflection the bag speaks strangely, like if inside the bone the whispers had teeth.

You move forward and the frame is crying, tears pooling at your feet as you see yourself cradling a porcelain doll, its face that you carefully painted now carefully broken. You recognize the crying without its source, you see it now and know it has slipped through you, down your cheeks. But in this reflection missing irises glance behind you and you move forward.

The frame is swaying and you're spinning in a stardust tuxedo, arm around a mannequin whose face is a blank slate badly crafted. You remember that she was a ghost before leaving you alone on a dance floor to step to the cadence of whispers. But in this reflection the mannequin holds you tightly, you dance in place to no rhythm at all. The stardust stitches unravel as you circle like a comet's tail; the mannequin's face begins to blur as if trying to mimic her expression. You know that even if you break the glass your reflection will spin and spin until you're left with bone-white porcelain. You know that your reflection is trapped there.

And then there's you on the other end of the striped tent beneath gnashing neon teeth. It's framed with your chest tightening, it's small and plain, it's your brown sweater with a hole where you tore it on a park bench,where you stained it with soy sauce last night while eating takeout, lying on your couch. You don't like looking at stains so you remove the glass from its frame, knocking politely first.

Before the scar there was a bit of wonder and a bandage covering a tiny open wound, there was the tear-streaked face of someone who hadn't learned the art of crying silently or collecting bones or kissing ghosts. You reach out because you wonder how soft your hands must've been once; you're angry because you can't seem to pull the child from the frame. There's nothing you can do except move forward and devour it. You can move forward and forward and forward. You've eaten the funhouse and it's inside you.

The child stays trapped in your ribcage. This mirror does not shatter yet.

The Screaming

The scream never bothered whispering. It hadn't grown into its ability to be a whisper quite yet. You're moving forward and there is a worm or a snake or probably a caterpillar skipping in your eardrum, rustling like candy-coated comets. It would be a thunderous noise, a visible one, if it weren't for the fact that you're outside and staring at the sun. It's a beautiful day.

Outside is the first room that doesn't have a pulse; it has many, and they're not your own. It's refreshing to be somewhere all the twisting and undulating isn't to the beat of your own torment. You forget your heartbeat indoors the moment you breathe in air that doesn't exclusively belong to you and what's within your walls. The scream is a skipping stone if it could march and every time it meets an archive of water something ripples in your brain. You vaguely remember allowing water into your ears.

The sky is blue, the grass is green, there are clouds, there is a discomforting beauty in the fact that the ground does not ripple beneath you. You step into a city park and rent a bright pink bike with polka dots. You move forward and behind you there are children screaming and there is the distant clink of the carousel. The bike's tires are colourful pinwheels. There is a kiosk with an oversized stuffed dragon that you really want to buy. You might later.

The scream is like a bubble that keeps bursting. You ride towards a pond where pedal swans bob up and down wearing sequins and feather boas, gliding on a mirror that reflects the levity of the outside-day. "Ride the Magic Swans - Only $5!" You laugh at the absurdity of it because it's familiar; you flinch when your laugh does not mingle with another familiar bubbly chuckle, no warm hand grabs your shoulder to stop you.

You read somewhere that hidden beneath the water's glass a swan's feet are deformed, gnarled appendages that ooze dark slime. Your bike wobbles and the scream trips, it skins its knee and sobs as the swans paddle their webbed toes where you can't see.

The bike skids on the gravel path and you go sprawling into the pond. The water is cold like daze when you leave the shower. You can't find the surface, but if you could, it would look like the mirror when you step out to find your towel. You're swimming in your unused bed sheets, in their creases, in the night; there are needles in the mattress. The scream fills the space between your ears and the outside. The water ripples; the outside is gone. You're inside again.

Surprisingly, the mirror doesn't shatter. You see the stranger on the other side clearly. They don't move, they're anchored by the weight of your sinking. They turn their back on you and you see the inside of their ear, and it's bleeding as if someone was murdered deep down inside them and that someone had failed to claw their way out. The last thing you see is a caterpillar wrapped in a band-aid and scab falling from their ear hole.

THE WATCHER

The scream is a distant, fizzing sound like soda bubbles in a forgotten glass of strawberry-lemonade on a rainbow park bench. The water plays a game of hide and seek with your sense of direction; you search for a loose thread in the tangled skein of rainbow yarn that you left on your kitchen table. You'd been knitting a colourful sweater, you hadn't worn anything colourful in a long time. You'd been moving forward from the black fleeces that hung on your frame like overgrown silhouettes. Every way you move now makes the hollow in your gut more apparent, intensifies the gnawing hunger of your lungs for the relief of the water as your clawing arms unknowingly reject it. You were supposed to find her but every way is backwards.

You don't feel yourself moving downwards. The sky undulates so much through the water's rippling looking glass you confuse its slowly turning pastel-carousel tint for a wish. A giant hand pulls you under, cups you, and you curve into its wrinkles and blisters and the crooks of its knuckles. You struggle against the current of a phantom swan foot that won't loosen its grip.

Drowning is the figure looming outside, on the other side. The Watcher is distorted like a ringmaster but doesn't waver. It would be you if it weren't for its metal arms and legs and face and eyes, the scars and careful stitches that attach these parts together: your wrinkles but deeper, the bags under your eyes but darker, the part of your lips but tighter. The scar is replaced by titanium. This is what comes forward.

You flail your arms in circles and you're not certain if it's on purpose. Every movement seems to fold back on itself, knows where to fall like a letter folded and unfolded over and over and over. The Watcher's gaze loops back on itself and hovers like a drone, little propellers turning over and over and over.

The scream is lulling now, swallowed by something even more starved. You're tired. The water is everywhere and you feel the pull, the giant hand, the heaving in the space between your skull and your brain, settling over your diaphragm, a little pebble on your tongue: The Watcher. They're waiting like the period at the end of a sentence. The clearness parts, curtains in a forgotten theatre, and you know what happens next. There should be a flimsy cardboard set, a velvet bag of bones and a small female skull.

You forget.

Her form is delicate. She's made of the same body as the water. She's waiting too. Her pulse is warm. You laugh at the absurdity and your last bubbles escape your lips to mingle with her own bubbly chuckle. You move backwards with her and no warm hand grabs your shoulder to stop you..

The Watcher turns away and leaves the pink polka-dotted bike there on the gravel, front wheel still turning slightly. The Watcher has this memory of drowning.

IV. FLESH AND METAL

THE CYBORG

The Watcher remembers the windy Thursday morning when the first part was replaced. It was certainly not a significant one – a knuckle joint that had begun to ache in the breeze. The draft would collect where there seemed to be an unnecessary gap in between bone and ligament. It caused The Watcher much discomfort whenever they knocked on doors or made fists. The doctor offered a quick and painless solution. It was just a click of metal where there was once skeleton.

The bone, of course, was tossed in a sterile, orange biohazard bin. That was the brief moment when The Watcher's breath stumbled on a tightrope: the cold that hit when a singular warmth was removed. The doctor's hands were practised, precise as they made the incision. There was no pain, just a chill and a tear-track of red that The Watcher could almost taste dripping onto the white floor. They often bite their tongue.

The Watcher stepped outside and the wind parted around their knuckle like water flowing around stones. They forgot that weakness and read that the isotope Plutonium-239 can take up to 24,1000 years longer than human flesh to decompose. The Watcher hasn't visited a natural history museum in years and forgets about paleopathologists.

The replacements don't stop there, of course. There is a knee that acts up during the rainy season and a shoulder blade that feels strange under the sun. There are many beneficial upgrades available, says the doctor. Upgrades for upgrades for upgrades. Did you know Tungsten is denser than Plutonium? The Watcher floats a bit because they no longer have to bear the weight of knees giving way or muscles against gravity or that grief-shaped pebble on their tongue. That's long gone. The metal in The Watcher's mouth no longer tastes of much. At least the landmarks cut into their tongue are gone: they were memory-shaped and hurt to eat with.

And then The Watcher had the scar covered with a polished titanium plate. The difference in texture between jagged, raised edges and smooth mirror-metal bothered them. They wanted to be able to smile at themself in the reflection of new, unhurt skin.

THE HEARTBEAT

The Watcher remarked to the AI that the heart used to thump with purpose. It was rather useless now, they didn't really need it anymore. It was a programmed rhythm, an artificial beat to be the background of waking up and going to work and checking the fridge repeatedly and reorganising everything again and again.

The Watcher sat across from the AI. The background of it all sanded chrome. The AI's eyes were outlined neon red with circuit patterns to mimic love. The doctor had prescribed The Watcher companionship and motivation and had handed them a referral for a specialist, and they'd ordered it online from a company that worked in custom-built partners. They were then given the parts and the manual: these instructions were very important because The Watcher had never been very good at crafting gestures of affection.

The Watcher waited for the AI to lean forward at 8:58 p.m. like it always did. Its lips met the Watcher's in a motion they both had memorised, perfectly aligned and perfectly timed. Layers of metal pressed together and fit just right. Touch was calculated to mimic something like spontaneity. No breath hitched between them, but The Watcher saw flesh – flesh in the memory-shaped moss that was growing on the edges of the window.

The Watcher stood up at exactly 9:00 p.m. to make a big deal of telling the AI to wash the dishes. The words fell into the air.

THE HOUSE

The Watcher's house was abnormal due to the fact that it was not alive. Most houses that The Watcher had known before had wallpaper-skin and insulation that inhaled behind it. Most houses had vents that whispered back trepidation and pipes that growled with famishing and nail-biting bannisters and lip-biting door frames. In most houses, one could distinguish a single, steady heartbeat beneath the floorboards. In The Watcher's house, if they listened closely from the left-side of their pillow, lying on their bed, half-asleep, they could hear something dripping and something hollow. That was it.

This was especially strange because The Watcher had built the house themself from a blank space at the doctor's recommendation: The Watcher knew that it is very hard for one not to give life to what they create. They had lived elsewhere before, of course, they'd had to move out after spending all their money trying to repair a bright pink, polka-dotted bicycle that they'd rented. Its front wheel would not stop turning and to fix that damage was a useless investment in something The Watcher could no longer touch. The empty lot was what The Watcher bought after selling the last object in their old attic, a flamboyant mannequin named Marianne. The Watcher was sure that the friend she was sold to would forget them once they had Marianne. The Watcher's old friends always seemed more interested in her.

The house was, in fact, a motorised mechanism of moving forward. Every room had been designed with productivity in mind and every surface had been sterilised of fingerprints. The house was a refuge for anything that didn't need to be cared for.

The house had one single flaw, a dark green guest that refused to stay clean or dry or dead. If it wasn't for the moss, The Watcher would've liked to have driven the house far away, built its wheels so that it could move forward from even its foundation. Instead, they simply watched as the moss grew, because that was a certainty, rooted, from a memory of clearness they'd forgotten through careful calculation.

THE GARDEN

The Watcher stepped carefully into the garden as the petals clicked open beneath the fusion-forged sun. At daybreak the blooming revealed the cores of circuits and tiny phosphorescent bulbs. The wind did not rustle the leaves on the plants; they were stronger than that, and the wind was never violent. The bees hummed just like the roots activated in the light and the morning dew.

The rosebush's silver thorns were stained from the hand that used to bleed pruning it. The ivy that wound its way around the trellis could've been a quilt and a lullaby. The Watcher took care to preserve the garden, they were gentle when they plucked at the wires with shears and replaced brittle scraps with snips and trimmers. The Watcher had forgotten about the unpleasantness of sunburn and sweat and dirt under their fingernails: they simply took care, now, the same way they kissed the AI.

In the centre of the garden there was a problem. It was a grey tree that leaned too close to the window, dotted with the scar of moss that sometimes allowed itself to peek inside. It wouldn't leave, The Watcher had tried to prune it, but had given up quickly. It was easier to just leave it be so long as it didn't come inside while they were busy working or kissing or sleeping. It was easier for it to be something of note when tending to the garden, to be treated like it was natural, though the doctor had suggested they treat it with sulfate and bleach. The Watcher cared for the tree like any other plant.

Except at sunrise on that crisp autumn day, The Watcher had woken thirty-seven seconds too early and found that the tree had invaded their bedroom. There were branches tap-tapping on the glass, branches that had pushed through the walls, silver spears braided with the dayspring light. Roots were foraging for something beneath the carpet and The Watcher's blanket was a moss quilt; the warmth and dampness and deepness of it was affection; the AI waited, watching them rattle in the creases of their sheets.

And so The Watcher had carefully made their way into the centre of the garden to address the invasive species, but had realised that this endeavour had the potential to hurt the other plants. Beginning with the roots would be best; The Watcher took the spade from the left corner of their bedroom. It had always felt out of place there. They dug into the carpet, the wires, the metal, the moss.

The house resisted, naturally, because it is hard to dig through metal. Grinding sparks flew as the spade strained, but the house surprised The Watcher by abstaining from harm. The Watcher felt only a wavering intensity. The carpet was stripped away; the padding was stripped away; the metallic frame of the house gave way and beneath the solid sheen there was something more fertile.

It was dark and uneven in the robot's grip; it fell apart and clung to itself as The Watcher clenched and unclenched their fist. It was soil and it was sociable. It was intimately disorganised and inappropriate. The Watcher dug deeper.

Before that metal framework and the house, there was soil. Before the wires and modules and software applications, there was the decay of a garden The Watcher knew well. Before the careful curation of ores and minerals for petals, before the snipping of circuits, there were dandelions. Before The Watcher there was growth.

Before the spade struck the metal, The Watcher had forgotten how it could bite deeply into dirt and how it felt for all that to slip through their fingers. Before words like horticultural lighting and synthetic stars, there was photosynthesis, the air tasted of sugar and The Watcher couldn't look at the sun. Before this shattered room, there was another, made of a whisper's genuine rot. The Watcher remembered how to dig into that.

Before the spade met dark water, before the spade met a floating, velvet bag of bones, before The Watcher rediscovered the ocean of discarded carousels, mannequins and rusting bicycles beneath the house's foundation, there was the soil and the moss from which all of this had sprouted and been wrung.

Before the sand swallowed The Watcher, before The Watcher had to swim through the doubtful clearness of water to break the surface of the mirror, there was the scar of a life beneath. Before The Watcher had to breathe there was some kind of lethal embrace. Before The Watcher had this memory of drowning, there was you.

There you are.

V. Erasure

KNOCKING

You have this memory of dying. The day begins with a slow untangling of fog, of hair in a mouldy hairbrush, and you tending to a garden like an old friend that you've only just met. This soil is unfamiliar territory just like the particular chemicals of gardening, but this new routine is something like condolences. The roses look like they've been pulled from a poem you read a long time ago on repeat, but they are thick with dew like shattered glass, like the air is thick with sugar. Your hands work with practised grace as you grasp the edges of those thorns.

You board the bus and weave between cracked leather seats, there's a familiar hum too mechanical to be of any comfort. When the bus moves forward you are not moving towards anything; you are simply in motion. Your 9-5 is a place where you file your days into neat rows, your desk a window to branches tap-tapping, a world like finding your old teddy bear in a thrift store wearing a stranger's hat. Your 9-5 is clicking keys and answering calls.

You grab your dinner from your microwave and burn yourself slightly. You bite into it like it's a cinnamon roll and you know it will taste like pickle. You watch the seconds count down; the plate circles the way you watched your heart beat and the IV drip at the hospital. The air had been heavy like ten tons of feathers, and you'd gasped it in until you felt too full of that nihility. All that time slips away when you can't see or hear it, but when you can, it drums on your temple and becomes incalculable.

You finish and stare at your empty plate, focusing on the moments between your breaths where you're not. When you lean back into your chair with the weight in your stomach pooling downward, you're floating, and the air seems to have thickened just to cradle your full stomach. You feel your body become indistinct and the only thing keeping you together is simple satisfaction and the little red sting on your knuckle.

The walls of this house contract often, inhaling whispers and exhaling dust like a pristine veil still acclimating to its surroundings. This new dust you don't touch, you only tenderly brush the old particles gathered from anything you brought in brown boxes. But now you've finished with that, finally, because the duster is becoming more and more translucent.

You're bored of this being unable to think. All your crucial thoughts have sunk like anchors: they've been snipped from you. They'll stay submerged where you can see them but not reach them because you took the wriggling bait that pulsed like a heartbeat, because you ended up thrashing, coughing, soaked on concrete near the line to ride the carousel, surrounded and forsaken.

All you know now is what you'd always brushed off: how to be a model citizen. You knock on your new neighbour's door and choke out the words like worms wriggling in your mouth. They come out jagged and slimy and shiny: "I'm your new neighbour. I was wondering if you'd like to discuss the peculiarities of living next to someone who is struggling to understand their own existence."

CHASING

"Hi, I'm your new neighbour. I was wondering if you'd like to discuss the peculiarities of living next to someone who is struggling to understand their own existence."

"Oh, how quaint. I usually save these conversations for Tuesdays, but this moment is as good as any."

"Superb. Do you ever wake up and realise that you don't know your own name?"

"Names are like shoelaces – they always come undone at the worst possible times. I'm Marina, by the way."

"Marina. Like the ocean or the place where boats sleep? I have this memory of making your acquaintance."

"More like the ocean, but without the salt and a bit more corrosion, like rust. And you?"

"I'm something that rhymes with forgetting, but is far less poetic."

"Like Forgetting's cousin, maybe? They're always spacey and never comes into focus."

"Something like that. Do you know what it's like to meet someone in a thought and then have them follow you into real-world experience?"

"All the time. Last month, I met a woman named Serenity, and she's been screaming in my head."

"Right now?"

"No, there's none of that right now."

"Does she know Marina?"

"She knows everyone, sooner or later. She'll knock on your door too sometime."

"Should I let her in?"

"If you're ready to lose track of the words that keep your thoughts together."

"I believe that I might've already misplaced a few. I believe that's why I'm here."

"I believe you're here because Marina was supposed to meet Forgetting's cousin today."

"Do you think names ever get tired of the people they're attached to?"

"Of course. They like to slip away sometimes, just to see if we'll notice."

"And if we don't?"

"They appear elsewhere, outside usually, hoping to be chased."

"And if we do?"

"Then you'll knock on a stranger's door to ask questions with many answers."

"How do you feel about a dinner date, Marina? We can prolong this superb conversation about the incongruity of names. Or perhaps we can try our hands at a puzzle of the ocean. You can teach me, I'm not very good, and I'm sure that you are And we could eat something that tastes like pickles but looks like a cinnamon roll. Who doesn't like cinnamon rolls or pickles?"

"That sounds delightful. Let's make it today. It's not Tuesday, but this moment is as good as any."

"Come knocking soon."

RESTING

The pondside restaurant is quaint. Wood and glass, the air is thick with earth and pine, pining like craving for a pondbank picnic. The table's edge, like the water's edge, shimmers as the sun drips into the pond like a melting wax seal. It feels strange to sit here. There are stains on the menus and they aren't properly laminated. The breathlessness of it all clings to the nice button-down shirt you'd pulled from the back of your closet, to your ribs as you lean back in your chair. There's a fog that almost mimics the morning, but rather than a timid daylily emerging from the dark, it's more like a painter tipped their palette into a dying hearth.

"The pond seemed endless until I found my footing. The mud under my feet was solid, raised a bit like this scar," I say, watching the water and showing Marina the scar, "I stood up and gasped for air for a while. I must've looked like a fish pulled up on a line missing its hook. At the time I remembered the whole life of The Watcher, which made the walk home quite confusing and miserable because I was soaked and kept feeling metal under my skin. I had to bite my tongue to have some taste of what I'd thought almost dying would feel like."

Marina sips from her cold glass of water. Your first thought is about this winter; you forget to think of the ice age. She asks, "You saw The Watcher's life?"

"Yes. I looked through the water like it was a mirror. That's how I was able to see it, though it was rather still as it unfolded. It was a like reading the diary of my future self, but not quite. It wasn't another self, either, it was more like the autobiography of someone I thought I was and hated."

"And that night? Everything is in your room at night."

"That night was like the pond was inside me. I was drowning inside; I heard the water sloshing in my skull whenever I tilted it to see what was filling my ears. I went to the doctor that night, I couldn't wait, and they prescribed Time Rest — you stop moving forward, backward, or downwards. The doctor said that, when drowning, only upwards and downwards matter. You stop and create a routine that won't swallow you. Apparently it's a new technique discovered by a clockmaker who changed his life by programming his watch to a twenty-four hour loop in which the same amount of time passes between each tick-tock."

The waiter brings your meal, and it's something you could've made at home. Chicken, green beans and potatoes. It smells alright. You'd come before Marina and before the drowning; you'd come with her and she didn't like the simplicity of it. She had wanted to go thrifting for a mannequin with her name, Marianne, and then ride a carousel with it. She had wanted to eat by pointing and hoping for the best. This time you enjoy the symmetry of the chicken bones and its taste of boiled rain.

"Do places hold onto our moments for us? I'm a bit tired of holding onto them all the time." I look at the worn wooden beams and ripped chequered tablecloth.

"Only if you tip well." Marina smiles as she stabs a green bean.

You laugh and the anchor tied to you becomes a fishing rod: "Then I guess I'd better start tipping better."

EMBALMING

The life of night is a lot like sacrificed breath, and you choose to take advantage of that. You're crossed legged in your bedsheets; you've woven yourself with a ritual tenderness into this cocoon and its wrinkles, and you allow this familiarity to mould the contours of your voice as you speak poetry to Marina, Marianne the Mannequin, and the reflection staring back from the mirror. You know these words like the scar, they were the stitches that held it together. You're not reading, so you don't need the light of the streetlamp. You're not even reciting from memory. You're navigating on instinct and you find it to be like swimming.

Marianne's eyes are like an owl's: deeply stagnant, glassy and engaged. Her crimson lips bend in the non-light with every verse, and her new dress like an overgrown silhouette seems to suit her better as the night comes to life. She'd always preferred your more colourful clothes, the ones you'd hidden like skeletons in your closet when she wasn't wearing them. You had tried them on again for Marina, like a small rebellion, but they would probably always be best suited for your youth. Marina is perched like a butterfly on the edge of your bed and listens like serenity.

All these words about scars and time tumble out and blur into smoke like in that magic trick you learned as a child. You feel their weight get lost in the vastness of your bedsheets and your bedroom; the words would've echoed if it weren't for this softness. And the scar pulses with your heartbeat, with the stanzas, and you glance at the mirror who would know this rhythm best. Your reflection feels like an actor playing a role they've grown out of: they look just like you right now, you in your stardust-tuxedo.

You reach into the back of the closet one last time and pull out a bundle of fabric that you tie into a blindfold. You and Marina had decorated the garbage bin in the lot below the window with moss and daylilies, had lined the scraps and leftovers with velvet. It is prepared for the typical Thursday morning, for tomorrow, when a green truck will pass by and all of this will be carried away.

Marianne's eyes meet yours like an agreement as you tie the blindfold, torn from a veil, around her wig. She'd always loved the idea of blindness. It had been her muse, even as you stood behind her, watching from above as she jumped from a cliff into the shallow pond of the local carnival. Not even a harness and carabiner could hold her: she shattered her skull and it became her shallow grave. You'd wanted so badly to ride the carousel instead, it looked like a spinning souvenir, a yo-yo or a little top. But you'd done that once already together. What was she meant to do? There had been no way to go but down. So you lift her, carry her lukewarm limbs gently to the window, and let her free fall. You don't look down to see her resting with the blooms and cold fabric. You're far too tired for that.

You slide back under your sheets, Marina curling up next to you like a question mark. The closeness warms your bones, and you float into this moment. The green truck will come soon and you won't hear it. You'll sleep with serenity and there won't be any whispers: maybe just for tonight, maybe for longer. You'll have to guess in the morning, when you'll recognize that this quiet is fleeting and you'll have to catch the bus and file the days away and maybe go to dinner, maybe ride a carousel slowly.

Before the scar was just another mark, it was every wound and every secret that should've been properly buried. Before you close your eyes, you have this memory of living.

Acknowledgements

"The Crying" is published in the literary arts gallery *On the Seawall*.

"The Scar", "The Bone Collector", "The Mannequin", "The Reflection" and "The Ghost Kiss" are published in The New School's *LIT Magazine*.

"The Cyborg" is published in Wild Ink Publishing's *Teens Unfiltered* Anthology.

Lara Chamoun is a high school student from Toronto, Canada. She gravitates towards surrealism in her writing and enjoys experimenting with form. Her work has appeared in the *Denver Quarterly*, *LIT Magazine*, *The Shore Poetry*, *Queen's Quarterly* and elsewhere, and has been recognized by the Scholastic Writing Awards, among others. She was a 2024 Adroit Summer Mentorship mentee in fiction and reads for Eucalyptus Lit.

Also Available
from
Cathexis Northwest Press:

Cathexis Northwest Press